SQL Programming for Data Analysis

Roggie Clark

Copyright

Title: SQL Programming for Data Analysis
Author: Roggie Clark

Cover Design: Roggie Clark
Editing: Renee' Clark

Printed in the United States of America

Disclaimer

The views and opinions expressed in this publication are those of the author and do not necessarily reflect the official policies, positions, opinions, or viewpoints of any individual, company, organization, institution, agency, or entity referenced or mentioned within this work.

The author is not necessarily affiliated with, endorsed by, sponsored by, or compensated by any individuals, companies, organizations, brands, institutions, products, or services referenced within this publication unless specifically stated otherwise. Any examples, sample situations, stories, illustrations, or scenarios presented may be fictionalized or simplified for educational purposes. Any resemblance to actual persons, living or dead, businesses, or events is purely coincidental unless otherwise stated.

The information, ideas, strategies, concepts, techniques, opinions, suggestions, and educational materials contained in this publication are provided on an "as is" basis without warranties of any kind, either express or implied. While every effort has been made to provide accurate and current information, neither the author nor the publisher makes any representations or warranties regarding the completeness, accuracy, reliability, suitability, or applicability of the information presented.

This publication is intended solely for educational and informational purposes and should not be interpreted as professional advice of any kind, including but not limited to financial, investment, legal, tax, business, medical, mental health, educational, psychological, or other professional guidance. Readers should conduct their own independent research and consult appropriately qualified professionals before making decisions that may affect their finances, health, business, education, legal matters, personal circumstances, or other important areas of life.

Results, outcomes, and experiences may vary significantly among individuals. Neither the author nor the publisher guarantees any specific outcomes, results, earnings, performance improvements, personal achievements, or benefits resulting from the use of information contained in this publication.

By reading, accessing, or using this publication, you acknowledge and agree that the author and publisher shall not be held liable for any direct, indirect, incidental, consequential, financial, personal, emotional, or other damages, losses, or claims arising from the use, misuse, interpretation, or application of information contained within this publication. You assume full responsibility for any actions, decisions, and outcomes resulting from the use of this material.

Table of Contents

Introduction

Data is everywhere, but having data and understanding data are two very different things. A company might have thousands of customer records, years of sales transactions, product information, marketing results, and expense records stored in a database. Those records become valuable when someone can ask the right questions and find meaningful answers. **SQL**, or Structured Query Language, gives you a practical way to do exactly that. In this book, the focus is not simply learning SQL commands. It is learning how to use SQL as a tool for data analysis.

Why SQL Is So Useful for Data Analysis

Imagine you are given a database containing 500,000 sales transactions.

Looking at the individual records would not tell you very much. There is simply too much information.

Instead, you might want answers to questions such as:

- How much revenue did the business generate?
- Which products generated the most sales?
- Which month performed best?

- What was the average order value?
- Which customers purchased most frequently?
- Which product categories are growing?
- Are there unusual records that need investigation?

SQL allows you to turn questions like these into instructions a database can understand.

For example, suppose you want to calculate total sales:

```
SELECT SUM(total_amount)
FROM orders;
```

Instead of examining every order manually, the database performs the calculation.

Perhaps you want to see sales by product category:

```
SELECT category,
SUM(total_amount)
FROM sales
GROUP BY category;
```

Or maybe you only want orders worth more than $500:

```
SELECT *
FROM orders
WHERE total_amount > 500;
```

Each query begins with a question.

That distinction is important because **data analysis** is not simply about retrieving records. It is the process of examining information to answer questions, identify patterns, make comparisons, and develop useful insights.

SQL is particularly well suited to this because databases often contain far more information than someone could reasonably analyze by looking at individual rows.

Instead of asking the database to show you everything, you can ask it to show you what matters.

From Raw Data to Useful Questions

Consider a simple sales table:

```
order_id | product        |
category    | quantity | revenue
101      | Keyboard       |
Accessories | 2        | 79.98
102      | Monitor        |
Electronics | 1        | 199.99
103      | Mouse          |
Accessories | 3        | 74.97
104      | Monitor        |
Electronics | 2        | 399.98
```

```
105          | Laptop Stand   |
Office          | 1           | 32.50
```

These records are **raw data**.

They tell us what happened, but they do not automatically explain what the information means.

An analyst might begin asking questions.

Which category generated the most revenue?

```
SELECT category, SUM(revenue) AS
total_revenue
FROM sales
GROUP BY category
ORDER BY total_revenue DESC;
```

Which product sold the greatest number of units?

```
SELECT product, SUM(quantity) AS
units_sold
FROM sales
GROUP BY product
ORDER BY units_sold DESC;
```

What was the average revenue per transaction?

```
SELECT AVG(revenue) AS
average_revenue
FROM sales;
```

Notice how the same dataset can answer several different questions.

This is why learning SQL for analysis requires more than learning syntax.

You must also learn to determine **what question you are trying to answer**.

A useful analytical process looks like this:

```
Business Question
       |
Identify the Relevant Data
       |
Write the SQL Query
       |
Examine the Results
       |
Interpret What They Mean
       |
Reach a Useful Insight
```

Suppose someone asks:

"Are sales improving?"

Before writing SQL, you need to think about what that question actually means.

Are we comparing this month with last month?

This year with last year?

Total revenue?

Number of orders?

Units sold?

The quality of your analysis depends partly on the quality of the question.

SQL can calculate exactly what you request, but it cannot decide whether you asked the right question.

That responsibility belongs to the analyst.

How to Approach SQL With an Analytical Mindset

An **analytical mindset** means approaching data with curiosity, structure, and a willingness to investigate before reaching conclusions.

Instead of immediately writing a complicated query, begin with the problem.

Suppose a manager says:

"Our sales seem lower. Find out what is happening."

That is not yet a SQL query.

It is a starting point.

You might first ask:

```
Are total sales actually lower?

When did the decline begin?
```

```
Are all product categories
declining?

Is one product responsible for
most of the change?

Did the number of orders
decline?

Did the average order value
decline?
```

Each question could lead to another SQL query.

For example, sales by month:

```
SELECT month, SUM(revenue) AS
monthly_revenue
FROM sales
GROUP BY month
ORDER BY month;
```

Then sales by category:

```
SELECT category, SUM(revenue) AS
category_revenue
FROM sales
GROUP BY category
ORDER BY category_revenue DESC;
```

Then perhaps average order value:

```
SELECT AVG(revenue) AS
average_order_value
FROM sales;
```

One query leads to another because analysis is often an investigation.

You should also avoid assuming that every unusual number automatically represents an important discovery.

Suppose one month shows dramatically higher sales.

That could mean the business performed exceptionally well.

But it could also mean:

- a large one-time order occurred
- duplicate records exist
- a data-entry mistake was made
- the reporting period contains extra days
- a promotion temporarily increased sales

SQL helps you find patterns, but **interpretation** determines what those patterns might mean.

Throughout this book, we will therefore approach SQL from two directions.

First:

"What SQL technique do we need?"

Second:

"What analytical question does that technique help us answer?"

You will learn how to retrieve information with `SELECT`, narrow results with `WHERE`, organize them with `ORDER BY`, calculate metrics with aggregate functions, compare groups with `GROUP BY`, combine related tables with `JOIN`, analyze time periods, and eventually use more advanced tools such as subqueries, Common Table Expressions, and window functions.

But the commands themselves are not the final objective.

The objective is reaching useful conclusions from data.

By the end of the book, you should be able to look at a business or analytical question and begin breaking it into smaller questions that SQL can help answer.

Last Thoughts

SQL becomes much more powerful when you stop viewing it as a collection of database commands and start viewing it as a way to investigate questions. Raw records provide the starting information, SQL helps you retrieve and summarize what matters, and your analytical thinking helps turn those results into useful insights. As we move through the book, keep one question in mind before writing any query: **What am I trying to learn from the data?** In the next chapter, we will begin building that analytical process by looking more closely at database structure, translating business questions into data questions, and constructing useful `SELECT` queries.

Chapter 1: SQL and the Data Analysis Process

Data analysis begins before you write a query. You first need to understand how the information is organized, determine what question you are trying to answer, and identify which pieces of data can help answer it. SQL then becomes the tool that translates those questions into instructions a database can execute. In this chapter, we will establish that process by looking at database structure, turning ordinary business questions into data questions, and building analytical queries with `SELECT`.

Understanding Tables, Columns, Rows, and Data Types

Most SQL analysis begins with a **table**.

A table organizes related information into a structure made up of rows and columns.

Imagine a company has a table named `sales`:

```
sale_id | sale_date  |
customer_id | product      |
quantity | revenue
101     | 2026-01-05 | 2001
| Keyboard    | 2          | 79.98
```

```
102       | 2026-01-06 | 2002
| Monitor      | 1          |
199.99
103       | 2026-01-06 | 2003
| Mouse        | 3          | 74.97
104       | 2026-01-07 | 2001
| Monitor      | 2          |
399.98
105       | 2026-01-08 | 2004
| Laptop Stand| 1          | 32.50
```

Each **row** represents one record.

For example:

```
102 | 2026-01-06 | 2002 |
Monitor | 1 | 199.99
```

represents one sales transaction.

Each **column** describes a particular piece of information about those transactions.

The `product` column tells us what was sold.

The `quantity` column tells us how many units were sold.

The `revenue` column tells us how much revenue the transaction generated.

This distinction matters because SQL queries frequently reference columns directly.

For example:

```
SELECT product
FROM sales;
```

This asks the database for values from the `product` column.

We could request several columns:

```
SELECT product, quantity,
revenue
FROM sales;
```

Or request every column:

```
SELECT *
FROM sales;
```

The asterisk tells SQL to return all columns.

While `SELECT *` can be convenient when exploring a small dataset, analysts often benefit from requesting only the columns they actually need. Doing so makes the purpose of a query clearer and can reduce unnecessary data retrieval.

Another important part of database structure is the **data type**.

Different columns can contain different kinds of information.

Conceptually, our sales table contains information such as:

```
sale_id          INTEGER
sale_date        DATE
customer_id      INTEGER
product          TEXT
quantity         INTEGER
revenue          DECIMAL
```

The exact data types available depend on the database system being used, but the basic idea is consistent.

Numbers can be calculated.

Text can be searched and compared.

Dates can be used to analyze periods of time.

Understanding the type of information stored in a column helps you determine what kinds of analysis make sense.

For example, calculating this is meaningful:

```
SELECT SUM(revenue)
FROM sales;
```

But trying to calculate the sum of product names would not provide a useful result.

Before analyzing an unfamiliar database, take time to understand its structure.

Ask:

What does each table represent?

What does each row represent?

What does each column mean?

What type of information does each column contain?

A technically correct query can still produce a misleading analysis if you misunderstand the underlying data.

Turning Business Questions Into Data Questions

Someone working with data is rarely handed a perfectly written SQL request.

Instead, you might hear:

"Which products are doing best?"

"Are sales improving?"

"Who are our best customers?"

"Where are we spending the most money?"

These are **business questions**. Before SQL can answer them, they need to become more precise data questions.

Consider:

"Which products are doing best?"

What does "best" mean?

It could mean:

```
Highest revenue
Most units sold
Most orders
Highest average sale
Fastest growth
```

Each interpretation could produce a different result.

Suppose the actual question is:

"Which products generated the most revenue?"

Now we have something SQL can measure.

We need:

```
Product
Revenue
```

The analytical process becomes:

```
Business question:
Which products generated the
most revenue?

Needed data:
Product and revenue

Calculation:
Total revenue for each product
```

```
Desired result:
Products ranked from highest to
lowest revenue
```

Eventually, that reasoning can become a query such as:

```
SELECT product, SUM(revenue) AS
total_revenue
FROM sales
GROUP BY product
ORDER BY total_revenue DESC;
```

We will explore grouping and calculations more deeply later. For now, notice how the query came from defining the question first.

Consider another request:

"Who are our best customers?"

Again, "best" is unclear.

Perhaps we decide it means customers who generated the most revenue.

Our data question becomes:

"Which customer IDs have the highest total revenue?"

Or suppose a manager asks:

"Are sales declining?"

We need to define the comparison.

A better data question might be:

"How does monthly revenue compare across the last six months?"

Now we know that we need both dates and revenue.

This process prevents a common analytical mistake: answering a slightly different question from the one people actually care about.

It also helps you determine whether the database contains the information necessary to answer the question.

Imagine someone asks:

"Which customers are happiest with their purchases?"

But your database contains only:

```
customer_id
order_date
product
quantity
revenue
```

There is no satisfaction score, survey response, review, or other measure of customer happiness.

SQL cannot create information that was never collected.

You may be able to investigate related behavior, such as repeat purchases, but that is not automatically the same as customer satisfaction.

Good analysis includes recognizing what the available data can and cannot tell you.

Building Analytical Queries With SELECT

The `SELECT` statement is the foundation of SQL data analysis because it allows you to specify which information you want to retrieve.

The basic structure is:

```
SELECT column_name
FROM table_name;
```

For example:

```
SELECT product
FROM sales;
```

To retrieve multiple columns:

```
SELECT product, quantity,
revenue
FROM sales;
```

We can also rename columns in the results using an **alias**.

Suppose we write:

```
SELECT product AS product_name
FROM sales;
```

The original database column remains `product`, but the query result displays it as `product_name`.

Aliases become particularly useful with calculations.

For example:

```
SELECT SUM(revenue) AS
total_revenue
FROM sales;
```

Instead of receiving a result with a less descriptive calculation label, we identify it as `total_revenue`.

SQL can also perform calculations between columns.

Suppose a table contains:

```
product | quantity | unit_price
```

We could calculate revenue for each record:

```
SELECT
    product,
    quantity,
    unit_price,
    quantity * unit_price AS
revenue
```

```
FROM sales;
```

The calculation does not necessarily have to exist as a permanent database column. SQL can calculate it when the query runs.

Another useful tool is `DISTINCT`.

Imagine the `sales` table contains hundreds of transactions, but you only want to know which products appear in the dataset.

Instead of:

```
SELECT product
FROM sales;
```

which may return the same product many times, you could write:

```
SELECT DISTINCT product
FROM sales;
```

The results might be:

```
Keyboard
Monitor
Mouse
Laptop Stand
```

This is useful during early data exploration.

You might use similar queries to investigate categories:

```
SELECT DISTINCT category
```

```
FROM products;
```

Or customer locations:

```
SELECT DISTINCT state
FROM customers;
```

Simple SELECT queries can therefore help you understand an unfamiliar dataset before performing deeper analysis.

Suppose you receive access to a sales database you have never worked with before.

You might begin with:

```
SELECT *
FROM sales;
```

Then examine specific fields:

```
SELECT sale_date, product,
quantity, revenue
FROM sales;
```

Then investigate unique values:

```
SELECT DISTINCT product
FROM sales;
```

Then begin performing calculations:

```
SELECT SUM(revenue) AS
total_revenue
FROM sales;
```

The queries become more useful as your questions become more specific.

That is the central pattern we will continue using throughout the book:

```
Understand the data
       |
Define the question
       |
Identify the needed columns
       |
Write the query
       |
Review the results
       |
Decide what to investigate next
```

SQL analysis is often iterative. One result creates another question, and that question leads to another query.

You do not need to begin with the most complicated SQL statement possible. In many situations, starting with a simple query and gradually narrowing the analysis produces a clearer understanding of the data.

Last Thoughts

Strong SQL analysis starts with understanding what your data represents. Tables organize information, rows represent records, columns describe characteristics, and data types influence how those values can be analyzed. Once you understand the structure, you can translate broad business questions into specific questions that SQL can answer. `SELECT` provides the starting point for retrieving and exploring that information. In the next chapter, we will make those queries more precise by filtering records, sorting results, limiting what SQL returns, and identifying potential problems within a dataset.

Chapter 2: Filtering, Sorting, and Exploring Data

A useful data analysis rarely requires every record in a database. More often, you need to isolate a particular group, compare values, arrange results in a meaningful order, or investigate records that may indicate a problem. SQL provides straightforward tools for narrowing large datasets into smaller, more useful results. In this chapter, we will use conditions to filter information, organize query results, and perform basic checks for missing, duplicate, and unusual data.

Finding the Right Records With WHERE

The `WHERE` clause allows you to specify which records should be included in a query.

Suppose our `sales` table contains:

```
sale_id | product        |
category     | quantity | revenue
101     | Keyboard       |
Accessories | 2         | 79.98
102     | Monitor        |
Electronics | 1         | 199.99
```

```
103        | Mouse                |
Accessories | 3            | 74.97
104        | Monitor              |
Electronics | 2            | 399.98
105        | Laptop Stand    | Office
| 1          | 32.50
```

If we only want sales from the Electronics category, we can write:

```
SELECT *
FROM sales
WHERE category = 'Electronics';
```

Instead of returning every record, SQL returns only records that meet the condition.

We can use comparison operators with numerical information as well.

To find transactions generating more than $100 in revenue:

```
SELECT *
FROM sales
WHERE revenue > 100;
```

Other useful comparisons include:

```
=    Equal to
<>   Not equal to
>    Greater than
<    Less than
>=   Greater than or equal to
```

```
<=   Less than or equal to
```

Suppose we want transactions with revenue between $50 and $200:

```
SELECT *
FROM sales
WHERE revenue BETWEEN 50 AND
200;
```

We can also search for several possible values with IN:

```
SELECT *
FROM sales
WHERE category IN
('Electronics', 'Office');
```

Analytical questions often require multiple conditions.

SQL provides **AND** when all specified conditions must be true.

```
SELECT *
FROM sales
WHERE category = 'Electronics'
AND revenue > 200;
```

Here, a record must belong to Electronics and have revenue greater than $200.

OR allows either condition to be true:

```
SELECT *
```

```
FROM sales
WHERE category = 'Electronics'
OR category = 'Office';
```

Filtering can also work with text patterns.

The **LIKE** operator can help locate text matching a particular pattern.

For example:

```
SELECT *
FROM sales
WHERE product LIKE '%Monitor%';
```

The `%` acts as a wildcard, allowing other characters to appear before or after the word.

These tools make it possible to translate increasingly specific analytical questions into SQL.

Instead of:

"Show me the sales."

You can ask:

"Show me Electronics transactions worth more than $200."

That increased precision is one of the most valuable parts of working with SQL.

Sorting and Limiting Query Results

Finding the correct records is only part of the analysis. You may also need to arrange them so important values are easier to recognize.

ORDER BY sorts query results.

Suppose we want to see sales from the highest revenue to the lowest:

```
SELECT product, revenue
FROM sales
ORDER BY revenue DESC;
```

DESC means descending order.

The highest value appears first.

For the opposite order, use ASC:

```
SELECT product, revenue
FROM sales
ORDER BY revenue ASC;
```

ASC means ascending order and is commonly the default.

Sorting becomes especially useful when answering ranking questions.

For example:

"Which transactions generated the most revenue?"

```
SELECT sale_id, product, revenue
FROM sales
```

```
ORDER BY revenue DESC;
```

We may not need every result, however.

If we only want the five largest transactions, many SQL systems allow us to use **LIMIT**:

```
SELECT sale_id, product, revenue
FROM sales
ORDER BY revenue DESC
LIMIT 5;
```

This produces a simple top-five analysis.

The same pattern could identify the five lowest transactions:

```
SELECT sale_id, product, revenue
FROM sales
ORDER BY revenue ASC
LIMIT 5;
```

You can combine filtering, sorting, and limiting in a single query.

Suppose the question is:

"What are the three highest-revenue Electronics transactions?"

We could write:

```
SELECT product, revenue
FROM sales
WHERE category = 'Electronics'
```

```
ORDER BY revenue DESC
LIMIT 3;
```

Notice how the query follows a logical analytical process.

First, choose the information:

```
SELECT product, revenue
```

Then identify the table:

```
FROM sales
```

Then narrow the records:

```
WHERE category = 'Electronics'
```

Then sort the results:

```
ORDER BY revenue DESC
```

Finally, keep only the first three:

```
LIMIT 3
```

This is an example of several simple SQL tools working together to answer a much more specific question.

Sorting can also involve multiple columns.

Suppose we want results organized first by category and then by revenue:

```
SELECT category, product,
revenue
FROM sales
```

```
ORDER BY category ASC, revenue
DESC;
```

SQL first organizes records by category. Within each category, it arranges revenue from highest to lowest.

As datasets grow, sorting and limiting become useful exploration tools because they allow you to quickly examine the highest, lowest, newest, oldest, or otherwise most relevant records.

Identifying Missing, Duplicate, and Unusual Data

Before trusting the results of an analysis, it is important to consider the quality of the underlying information.

Real datasets can contain problems.

A customer may appear twice.

A transaction may be missing a value.

A price may have been entered incorrectly.

A quantity may be unusually high or low.

These issues can influence analytical results.

One common problem is a **NULL value**, which represents missing or unknown information in SQL.

Suppose some sales records do not contain revenue values.

We can locate them with:

```
SELECT *
FROM sales
WHERE revenue IS NULL;
```

To find records that do contain revenue:

```
SELECT *
FROM sales
WHERE revenue IS NOT NULL;
```

It is important to use `IS NULL` rather than:

```
WHERE revenue = NULL;
```

NULL represents the absence of a known value, so SQL handles it differently from an ordinary number or piece of text.

Duplicates can create another problem.

Suppose a customer table contains the same email address several times.

We could investigate with:

```
SELECT email, COUNT(*) AS
occurrences
FROM customers
GROUP BY email
HAVING COUNT(*) > 1;
```

The query counts how many times each email occurs and returns those appearing more than once.

A result might look like:

```
email                |
occurrences
maya@example.com     | 2
carlos@example.com   | 3
```

That does not automatically mean the data is wrong. There could be a legitimate reason for repeated values.

The query tells us what needs investigation.

Analysts should also look for unusual values.

Suppose most orders generate between $20 and $500, but one transaction shows:

```
$95,000
```

We might investigate high values using:

```
SELECT sale_id, product, revenue
FROM sales
WHERE revenue > 5000
ORDER BY revenue DESC;
```

Again, an unusual value is not necessarily incorrect.

It could represent a legitimate large transaction.

The important point is that it deserves attention before being used in an analysis.

Negative values may also require investigation:

```
SELECT *
FROM sales
WHERE quantity < 0;
```

Depending on the dataset, a negative quantity could indicate a return, an adjustment, or a data-entry error.

Context matters.

We can perform similar checks for values outside expected ranges:

```
SELECT *
FROM products
WHERE price <= 0;
```

Or missing customer information:

```
SELECT *
FROM customers
WHERE email IS NULL;
```

These checks are part of **data quality** analysis.

SQL cannot automatically determine whether every unusual record is correct or incorrect. Instead, it helps you identify records that may deserve closer examination.

This distinction matters because removing unusual values without understanding them can damage an analysis just as easily as leaving incorrect data in place.

Suppose a business receives one unusually large order.

Deleting it simply because it is much larger than the other transactions would remove a legitimate sale.

A better analytical process is:

```
Find the unusual record
        |
Investigate why it is unusual
        |
Determine whether it is valid
        |
Decide how it should be handled
```

Filtering therefore serves two purposes.

It helps you find the records relevant to your question, and it helps you investigate the quality of the data itself.

Last Thoughts

Filtering and sorting allow you to move beyond simply retrieving records and begin focusing on the information that matters to a particular analysis. `WHERE` helps narrow a dataset, `ORDER BY` organizes the results, and `LIMIT` can focus attention on the most relevant records. SQL can also help uncover missing values, possible duplicates, and unusual observations before those issues affect your conclusions. In the next chapter, we will move from exploring individual records to calculating metrics, summarizing groups, and creating practical measurements that reveal what is happening across an entire dataset.

Chapter 3: Calculating Metrics and Summarizing Data

Individual records can tell you what happened one transaction at a time, but data analysis often requires a broader view. Instead of examining every sale separately, you may want to know total revenue, average order value, the number of customers, or which product category performs best. SQL can perform these calculations directly inside the database. In this chapter, we will use summary calculations, group records for comparison, and create practical measurements that make large datasets easier to understand.

Using COUNT, SUM, AVG, MIN, and MAX

SQL provides several functions for summarizing collections of values.

Suppose our `sales` table contains:

```
sale_id | product         |
category     | quantity | revenue
101     | Keyboard        |
Accessories | 2          | 79.98
```

```
102         | Monitor           |
Electronics | 1                 | 199.99
103         | Mouse             |
Accessories | 3                 | 74.97
104         | Monitor           |
Electronics | 2                 | 399.98
105         | Laptop Stand      | Office
| 1             | 32.50
```

One of the simplest analytical questions is:

"How many sales records are there?"

SQL can answer this using `COUNT()`:

```
SELECT COUNT(*) AS
number_of_sales
FROM sales;
```

The result would be:

```
number_of_sales
5
```

Suppose we want total revenue instead.

We can use `SUM()`:

```
SELECT SUM(revenue) AS
total_revenue
FROM sales;
```

SQL adds the revenue values together.

We can calculate the average with `AVG()`:

```
SELECT AVG(revenue) AS
average_revenue
FROM sales;
```

We can also find the smallest and largest values:

```
SELECT
    MIN(revenue) AS
lowest_revenue,
    MAX(revenue) AS
highest_revenue
FROM sales;
```

These calculations can be combined:

```
SELECT
    COUNT(*) AS number_of_sales,
    SUM(revenue) AS
total_revenue,
    AVG(revenue) AS
average_revenue,
    MIN(revenue) AS
lowest_revenue,
    MAX(revenue) AS
highest_revenue
FROM sales;
```

One query now provides a compact summary of the dataset.

These functions answer different analytical questions:

```
COUNT()   How many?
```

```
SUM()       How much in total?
AVG()       What is the average?
MIN()       What is the lowest
value?
MAX()       What is the highest
value?
```

We can also combine these calculations with filtering.

Suppose we only want to calculate revenue from Electronics:

```
SELECT SUM(revenue) AS
electronics_revenue
FROM sales
WHERE category = 'Electronics';
```

Or perhaps we want the average revenue for transactions above $50:

```
SELECT AVG(revenue) AS
average_revenue
FROM sales
WHERE revenue > 50;
```

This is where SQL begins turning large collections of records into measurements that are much easier to interpret.

Comparing Categories With GROUP BY and HAVING

A total can tell us how the entire dataset performed, but analysts frequently need comparisons.

Suppose total revenue is $50,000.

That is useful, but it does not tell us which products or categories generated that revenue.

GROUP BY allows SQL to organize records into groups before performing calculations.

To calculate revenue for each category:

```
SELECT
    category,
    SUM(revenue) AS
total_revenue
FROM sales
GROUP BY category;
```

The result might look like:

```
category      | total_revenue
Accessories | 154.95
Electronics | 599.97
Office       | 32.50
```

Now we can compare categories.

We can make the comparison even clearer by sorting the results:

```
SELECT
    category,
```

```
    SUM(revenue) AS
total_revenue
FROM sales
GROUP BY category
ORDER BY total_revenue DESC;
```

The highest-revenue category appears first.

The same approach can answer many questions.

How many transactions involved each product?

```
SELECT
    product,
    COUNT(*) AS number_of_sales
FROM sales
GROUP BY product;
```

How many units of each product were sold?

```
SELECT
    product,
    SUM(quantity) AS units_sold
FROM sales
GROUP BY product
ORDER BY units_sold DESC;
```

What was the average transaction revenue for each category?

```
SELECT
    category,
    AVG(revenue) AS
average_revenue
```

```
FROM sales
GROUP BY category;
```

Sometimes we need to filter the groups after the calculations have been performed.

For this, SQL provides `HAVING`.

Suppose we only want categories generating more than $100 in total revenue:

```
SELECT
    category,
    SUM(revenue) AS
total_revenue
FROM sales
GROUP BY category
HAVING SUM(revenue) > 100;
```

It is useful to understand the difference between `WHERE` and **HAVING**.

`WHERE` filters individual records before they are grouped.

`HAVING` filters groups after the grouping and calculations occur.

For example:

```
SELECT
    category,
    SUM(revenue) AS
total_revenue
```

```
FROM sales
WHERE revenue > 50
GROUP BY category
HAVING SUM(revenue) > 100;
```

First:

```
WHERE revenue > 50
```

removes individual transactions worth $50 or less.

Then:

```
GROUP BY category
```

organizes the remaining records by category.

Finally:

```
HAVING SUM(revenue) > 100
```

keeps only groups whose total revenue exceeds $100.

This sequence is important because filtering records and filtering calculated groups are not the same analytical operation.

Creating Calculated Values and Practical KPIs

Not every useful measurement already exists as a column in a database.

Sometimes analysts need to calculate new values from existing information.

Suppose an `order_items` table contains:

```
product        | quantity |
unit_price
Keyboard       | 2          | 39.99
Monitor        | 1          |
199.99
Mouse          | 3          | 24.99
Laptop Stand   | 2          | 32.50
```

If there is no revenue column, we can calculate one:

```
SELECT
    product,
    quantity,
    unit_price,
    quantity * unit_price AS
revenue
FROM order_items;
```

The expression:

```
quantity * unit_price
```

creates a calculated value for each record.

We can also calculate total revenue:

```
SELECT
    SUM(quantity * unit_price)
AS total_revenue
FROM order_items;
```

These calculations can become **Key Performance Indicators**, commonly called KPIs.

A KPI is a measurement used to evaluate some aspect of performance.

For example, a business might track total revenue:

```
SELECT SUM(revenue) AS
total_revenue
FROM sales;
```

Another useful measurement is average order value.

Suppose an `orders` table contains one record per completed order:

```
SELECT AVG(order_total) AS
average_order_value
FROM orders;
```

If we instead need to calculate it from total revenue and the number of orders, we might use:

```
SELECT
    SUM(order_total) / COUNT(*)
AS average_order_value
FROM orders;
```

A business could also measure the number of unique customers who purchased:

```
SELECT COUNT(DISTINCT
customer_id) AS
purchasing_customers
FROM orders;
```

This is different from:

```
SELECT COUNT(*) AS
number_of_orders
FROM orders;
```

A customer may place multiple orders, so the number of orders and the number of unique customers can represent very different things.

Suppose there are:

```
1,000 orders
650 unique customers
```

Those two measurements answer different questions.

SQL can also calculate percentages.

Imagine a `customers` table containing a `status` column with values such as `Active` and `Inactive`.

We could calculate the percentage of active customers:

```
SELECT
    100.0 * SUM(
        CASE
            WHEN status =
'Active' THEN 1
            ELSE 0
        END
```

```
    ) / COUNT(*) AS
active_customer_percentage
FROM customers;
```

Here, CASE allows SQL to apply conditional logic inside the calculation.

Each active customer contributes 1, while other customers contribute 0.

That total is divided by the number of customer records and converted into a percentage.

Analysts can use this type of logic to create many practical measurements.

For example:

```
Total revenue
Average order value
Number of orders
Unique customers
Units sold
Revenue per customer
Conversion percentage
Return percentage
Average transaction size
```

However, calculating a number does not automatically make it a useful KPI.

A useful measurement should connect to a meaningful question.

If the question is:

"Are customers spending more when they order?"

Average order value might be useful.

If the question is:

"Are we attracting more buyers?"

The number of unique purchasing customers may be more relevant.

If the question is:

"Which product contributes most to sales?"

Revenue grouped by product could provide a better answer.

This is why SQL analysis should continue to begin with the question rather than the calculation.

A database may allow you to calculate hundreds of different metrics. The analytical skill is determining which measurements actually help explain the problem you are investigating.

Last Thoughts

Summary calculations transform individual database records into information that is easier to compare and interpret. `COUNT()`, `SUM()`, `AVG()`, `MIN()`, and `MAX()` answer fundamental questions about a dataset, while `GROUP BY` allows those calculations to be compared across products, customers, categories, or other groups. `HAVING` provides another level of filtering, and calculated values can turn existing fields into practical KPIs. In the next chapter, we will expand the analysis beyond a single table by connecting related information and using JOINs to answer questions that depend on multiple parts of a database.

Chapter 4: Combining Data From Multiple Tables

Many analytical questions cannot be answered using a single table. Customer information may be stored separately from orders, while product information may exist in another table entirely. SQL allows these related records to be brought together when they share meaningful identifiers. In this chapter, we will look at how tables are connected, use JOINs to analyze related data, and combine multiple sources of database information to answer practical business questions.

Understanding Keys and Table Relationships

Consider an online store with three tables:

```
customers
orders
products
```

The `customers` table might contain:

```
customer_id | customer_name |
state
```

```
1001          | Maya Johnson   |
Maryland
1002          | Carlos Smith   |
Virginia
1003          | Aisha Brown    |
Georgia
```

The `orders` table might contain:

```
order_id | customer_id |
product_id | quantity |
order_total
501       | 1001          | 201
| 2          | 79.98
502       | 1002          | 202
| 1          | 199.99
503       | 1001          | 203
| 3          | 74.97
504       | 1003          | 202
| 2          | 399.98
```

The `products` table might contain:

```
product_id | product_name |
category
201          | Keyboard       |
Accessories
202          | Monitor        |
Electronics
203          | Mouse          |
Accessories
```

These tables contain different types of information, but they are connected.

The `customer_id` in `customers` identifies each customer. The same value appears in `orders`, allowing us to determine which customer placed each order.

Similarly, `product_id` connects orders to products.

These connections are called **table relationships**.

A common relationship is **one-to-many**.

One customer can place many orders:

```
Customer 1001
      |
      |---- Order 501
      |
      |---- Order 503
```

The customer exists once in the `customers` table but can be referenced by many records in `orders`.

This structure avoids unnecessarily repeating the customer's information in every order.

Instead of storing:

```
501 | Maya Johnson | Maryland |
Keyboard | 79.98
```

```
503 | Maya Johnson | Maryland |
Mouse      | 74.97
```

the database can store the customer once and reference that customer through an ID.

Understanding these relationships is important for analysis because the information needed to answer a question may be spread across several tables.

Suppose you are asked:

"Which states generated the most revenue?"

The `orders` table contains revenue information, but it does not contain the customer's state.

The `customers` table contains the state, but it does not contain order totals.

Neither table can answer the question alone.

We need to connect them.

Analyzing Related Data With JOINs

A **JOIN** allows SQL to combine related records from different tables.

Suppose we want to see each customer's name alongside their orders.

We can write:

```
SELECT
    customers.customer_name,
    orders.order_id,
    orders.order_total
FROM customers
JOIN orders
ON customers.customer_id =
orders.customer_id;
```

The important part is:

```
ON customers.customer_id =
orders.customer_id
```

This tells SQL how the records are related.

The result might look like:

```
customer_name | order_id |
order_total
Maya Johnson  | 501      | 79.98
Carlos Smith  | 502      |
199.99
Maya Johnson  | 503      | 74.97
Aisha Brown   | 504      |
399.98
```

Now information from two tables appears in one result.

The type of JOIN used here is an **INNER JOIN**. Writing `JOIN` commonly means the same thing as `INNER JOIN`.

We could write it explicitly:

```
SELECT
    customers.customer_name,
    orders.order_total
FROM customers
INNER JOIN orders
ON customers.customer_id =
orders.customer_id;
```

An INNER JOIN returns records where matching values exist in both tables.

This works well when we only want customers who have matching orders.

But what if we want to see every customer, including customers who have never ordered?

We can use a **LEFT JOIN**:

```
SELECT
    customers.customer_name,
    orders.order_id,
    orders.order_total
FROM customers
LEFT JOIN orders
ON customers.customer_id =
orders.customer_id;
```

The customers from the left table are retained even when no matching order exists.

This can answer useful analytical questions.

For example:

"Which customers have never placed an order?"

```
SELECT
    customers.customer_id,
    customers.customer_name
FROM customers
LEFT JOIN orders
ON customers.customer_id =
orders.customer_id
WHERE orders.order_id IS NULL;
```

The JOIN combines the tables, while the WHERE condition identifies customers without a matching order.

JOINs can also be combined with the calculations you learned earlier.

Suppose we want total revenue by customer:

```
SELECT
    customers.customer_name,
    SUM(orders.order_total) AS
total_revenue
FROM customers
JOIN orders
ON customers.customer_id =
orders.customer_id
GROUP BY customers.customer_id,
customers.customer_name
```

```
ORDER BY total_revenue DESC;
```

Now several SQL concepts are working together.

`JOIN` connects customers and orders.

`SUM()` calculates revenue.

`GROUP BY` creates a result for each customer.

`ORDER BY` ranks customers by total revenue.

This allows us to answer:

"Which customers generated the most revenue?"

Using Multiple Tables to Answer Business Questions

The real value of JOINs becomes clearer when an analytical question requires information from several parts of a database.

Suppose we want to know:

"Which product categories generate the most revenue?"

Our order information contains:

```
product_id
order_total
```

Our product information contains:

```
product_id
product_name
category
```

We can combine them:

```
SELECT
    products.category,
    SUM(orders.order_total) AS
total_revenue
FROM orders
JOIN products
ON orders.product_id =
products.product_id
GROUP BY products.category
ORDER BY total_revenue DESC;
```

The result might look like:

```
category    | total_revenue
Electronics | 599.97
Accessories | 154.95
```

Now suppose we want to answer:

"Which states generated the most revenue?"

That requires customer and order information:

```
SELECT
    customers.state,
    SUM(orders.order_total) AS
total_revenue
FROM customers
```

```
JOIN orders
ON customers.customer_id =
orders.customer_id
GROUP BY customers.state
ORDER BY total_revenue DESC;
```

We can go further and use all three tables.

Suppose the question becomes:

"Which product categories are generating the most revenue in each customer state?"

We need:

```
customers -> state
orders    -> customer_id,
product_id, order_total
products  -> category
```

The query can connect all three:

```
SELECT
    customers.state,
    products.category,
    SUM(orders.order_total) AS
total_revenue
FROM orders
JOIN customers
ON orders.customer_id =
customers.customer_id
JOIN products
```

```
ON orders.product_id =
products.product_id
GROUP BY customers.state,
products.category
ORDER BY customers.state,
total_revenue DESC;
```

This illustrates why understanding the database structure is so important.

Before writing the query, determine where each required piece of information lives.

For example:

```
Question:
Which product categories
generate the most revenue by
state?

Need:
State
Category
Revenue

State comes from:
customers

Category comes from:
products
```

```
Revenue comes from:
orders

Connections:
customers.customer_id =
orders.customer_id
products.product_id =
orders.product_id
```

Once those relationships are clear, the SQL becomes easier to construct.

This approach also helps prevent incorrect JOINs.

Suppose two unrelated tables both happen to contain an `id` column. That does not mean those columns should be joined.

A JOIN should represent an actual relationship in the data.

Incorrect relationships can create misleading results, duplicate records, or inflated calculations.

This is especially important when calculating totals.

If a JOIN unexpectedly creates multiple copies of the same transaction, a calculation such as:

```
SUM(orders.order_total)
```

could produce a total much larger than the real amount.

When working with multiple tables, check your results.

You might compare:

```
SELECT COUNT(*)
FROM orders;
```

with the number of records produced after a JOIN.

You can also inspect a smaller result before calculating totals:

```
SELECT
    orders.order_id,
    customers.customer_name,
    products.product_name,
    orders.order_total
FROM orders
JOIN customers
ON orders.customer_id =
customers.customer_id
JOIN products
ON orders.product_id =
products.product_id
LIMIT 20;
```

Looking at the joined records can help you confirm that the relationships behave as expected before building more complicated analysis on top of them.

This is an important analytical habit.

Do not assume that a query is correct simply because it runs successfully.

A SQL statement can execute without an error and still answer the wrong question.

Understand the relationships, inspect the results, and make sure the numbers make sense before drawing conclusions from them.

Last Thoughts

JOINs allow you to move beyond isolated tables and analyze relationships across a database. Keys provide the connections between customers, orders, products, and other records, while INNER JOINs and LEFT JOINs give you different ways to decide which matching and nonmatching records should appear. As analytical questions become more complex, identifying where the necessary information is stored becomes just as important as writing the SQL itself. In the next chapter, we will build on these skills by analyzing changes over time and using subqueries, Common Table Expressions, and window functions to create more advanced analytical queries.

Chapter 5: Analyzing Trends and Building Advanced Queries

Many analytical questions involve more than calculating a total or comparing categories. You may need to understand how performance changes from one period to another, compare a current result with an earlier result, rank products, or organize a complicated analysis into smaller steps. SQL provides several tools for these situations. In this chapter, we will work with dates and time periods, organize more complex analysis with subqueries and Common Table Expressions, and introduce window functions for rankings, comparisons, and trends.

Working With Dates and Changes Over Time

Time is one of the most important dimensions in data analysis.

A business may know that it generated $500,000 in revenue, but that number becomes more meaningful when it can be compared with another period.

For example:

```
January revenue:  $42,000
February revenue: $47,000
March revenue:    $55,000
```

Now we can see that revenue has been increasing.

Suppose our `orders` table contains:

```
order_id | order_date |
customer_id | order_total
501      | 2026-01-08 | 1001
| 79.98
502      | 2026-01-15 | 1002
| 199.99
503      | 2026-02-04 | 1003
| 74.97
504      | 2026-02-18 | 1001
| 399.98
505      | 2026-03-02 | 1004
| 132.50
```

We might begin by filtering for a particular period.

For example:

```
SELECT *
FROM orders
WHERE order_date >= '2026-02-01'
AND order_date < '2026-03-01';
```

This retrieves orders from February 2026.

The exact functions available for extracting years, months, and other portions of dates vary between database systems. For example, some systems provide functions such as `YEAR()` and `MONTH()`, while SQLite commonly uses `strftime()`.

In SQLite, monthly revenue could be calculated with:

```
SELECT
    strftime('%Y-%m',
order_date) AS month,
    SUM(order_total) AS
monthly_revenue
FROM orders
GROUP BY strftime('%Y-%m',
order_date)
ORDER BY month;
```

The result might look like:

```
month   | monthly_revenue
2026-01 | 279.97
2026-02 | 474.95
2026-03 | 132.50
```

This is an example of **time-series analysis**, where values are examined across time.

The same idea can be used to analyze:

```
Daily sales
Weekly orders
Monthly revenue
```

```
Quarterly expenses
Annual customer growth
```
Dates can also help answer questions about specific periods.

Suppose we want orders placed after July 1:

```
SELECT *
FROM orders
WHERE order_date >=
'2026-07-01';
```
Or perhaps we want to compare yearly performance:

```
SELECT
    strftime('%Y', order_date)
AS year,
    SUM(order_total) AS
total_revenue
FROM orders
GROUP BY strftime('%Y',
order_date)
ORDER BY year;
```
Simply seeing values over time can reveal useful patterns.

For example:

```
2023 | $420,000
2024 | $465,000
2025 | $510,000
```

```
2026 | $548,000
```

There appears to be an upward trend.

But analysts should be careful when interpreting time-based information.

A single strong month does not necessarily mean long-term growth.

Seasonality can also affect comparisons.

For example, a retailer may consistently generate more revenue during the holiday season. Comparing December directly with January without considering that pattern could produce a misleading conclusion.

When analyzing changes over time, ask:

```
What periods am I comparing?

Are the periods comparable?

Is there a seasonal pattern?

Is the change temporary or
persistent?

Did something unusual happen
during the period?
```

SQL can calculate the numbers, but understanding their context remains part of the analysis.

Organizing Analysis With Subqueries and Common Table Expressions

As analytical questions become more complicated, a single query can become difficult to read.

One way to break a problem into smaller pieces is with a **subquery**.

A subquery is a query placed inside another query.

Suppose we want to find orders worth more than the average order.

First, we can calculate the average:

```
SELECT AVG(order_total)
FROM orders;
```

Then we can place that calculation inside another query:

```
SELECT
    order_id,
    customer_id,
    order_total
FROM orders
WHERE order_total > (
    SELECT AVG(order_total)
    FROM orders
);
```

The inner query calculates the average order value.

The outer query finds orders greater than that average.

This allows SQL to answer a question that depends on another calculated result.

Subqueries can be useful, but large nested queries can become difficult to follow.

Another option is a **Common Table Expression**, often shortened to CTE.

A CTE creates a temporary named result that can be referenced by the main query.

It begins with `WITH`.

For example:

```
WITH customer_sales AS (
    SELECT
        customer_id,
        SUM(order_total) AS
total_spent
    FROM orders
    GROUP BY customer_id
)

SELECT
    customer_id,
    total_spent
FROM customer_sales
```

```
ORDER BY total_spent DESC;
```

The first section:

```
WITH customer_sales AS (
    SELECT
        customer_id,
        SUM(order_total) AS
total_spent
    FROM orders
    GROUP BY customer_id
)
```

creates a temporary result named `customer_sales`.

The second section analyzes that result.

This can make a complex analytical process easier to understand.

Suppose we only want customers who spent more than $1,000:

```
WITH customer_sales AS (
    SELECT
        customer_id,
        SUM(order_total) AS
total_spent
    FROM orders
    GROUP BY customer_id
)
```

```
SELECT
    customer_id,
    total_spent
FROM customer_sales
WHERE total_spent > 1000
ORDER BY total_spent DESC;
```

The logic becomes:

```
Step 1:
Calculate spending for each
customer.

Step 2:
Keep customers who spent more
than $1,000.

Step 3:
Rank them by spending.
```

This step-by-step structure can make analytical SQL easier to build and troubleshoot.

Instead of trying to solve a large problem all at once, create smaller results and then build on them.

Using Window Functions for Rankings, Comparisons, and Trends

Sometimes you want to perform calculations across related rows without reducing those rows into a single grouped result.

This is where **window functions** become useful.

Suppose we calculate revenue by product:

```
product         | total_revenue
Monitor         | 12500
Keyboard        | 8400
Mouse           | 7200
Laptop Stand    | 5100
```

We might want to assign each product a ranking.

The RANK( ) window function can do this:

```
SELECT
    product,
    total_revenue,
    RANK() OVER (
        ORDER BY total_revenue
DESC
    ) AS revenue_rank
FROM product_sales;
```

The result might be:

```
product         | total_revenue |
revenue_rank
Monitor         | 12500         |
1
Keyboard        | 8400          |
2
Mouse           | 7200          |
3
```

```
Laptop Stand   | 5100              |
4
```

The `OVER()` portion defines the group of records the window function works across.

Window functions can also perform calculations within categories.

Suppose products belong to several categories. We might want to rank products inside each category:

```
SELECT
    category,
    product,
    total_revenue,
    RANK() OVER (
        PARTITION BY category
        ORDER BY total_revenue
DESC
    ) AS category_rank
FROM product_sales;
```

`PARTITION BY` creates separate analytical groups without collapsing the individual records.

This could help answer:

"What is the highest-performing product within each category?"

Another useful window function is `LAG()`.

`LAG()` allows a row to reference a value from an earlier row.

Suppose monthly revenue is:

```
month   | revenue
2026-01 | 42000
2026-02 | 47000
2026-03 | 55000
```

We can retrieve the previous month's revenue:

```
SELECT
    month,
    revenue,
    LAG(revenue) OVER (
        ORDER BY month
    ) AS previous_month_revenue
FROM monthly_sales;
```

The result might be:

```
month   | revenue |
previous_month_revenue
2026-01 | 42000   | NULL
2026-02 | 47000   | 42000
2026-03 | 55000   | 47000
```

Now we can calculate the change:

```
SELECT
    month,
    revenue,
```

```
    revenue - LAG(revenue) OVER
(
        ORDER BY month
    ) AS revenue_change
FROM monthly_sales;
```

The result could become:

```
month    | revenue |
revenue_change
2026-01 | 42000   | NULL
2026-02 | 47000   | 5000
2026-03 | 55000   | 8000
```

We can even calculate percentage change:

```
SELECT
    month,
    revenue,
    100.0 * (
        revenue - LAG(revenue)
OVER (ORDER BY month)
    ) / LAG(revenue) OVER (ORDER
BY month)
    AS percent_change
FROM monthly_sales;
```

Window functions can also create running totals.

Suppose we want cumulative revenue:

```
SELECT
    month,
```

```
    revenue,
    SUM(revenue) OVER (
        ORDER BY month
    ) AS running_revenue
FROM monthly_sales;
```

The result might look like:

```
month    | revenue |
running_revenue
2026-01 | 42000    | 42000
2026-02 | 47000    | 89000
2026-03 | 55000    | 144000
```

These techniques allow SQL to answer more sophisticated analytical questions:

```
Which product ranks first?

How did this month compare with
last month?

How much has revenue changed?

What is the cumulative total?

Which product ranks highest
within each category?
```

Window functions may initially look more complicated than basic SQL, but the analytical idea is straightforward.

You are asking SQL to perform calculations across related records while still preserving the individual rows needed for comparison.

You do not need to memorize every window function. Start by understanding what you want to compare, then determine whether ranking, previous-period comparison, or a running calculation can help answer the question.

Last Thoughts

Time-based analysis allows you to move from understanding what happened to understanding how results are changing. Subqueries and Common Table Expressions make it easier to divide complicated analytical questions into manageable pieces, while window functions provide powerful tools for rankings, previous-period comparisons, and running calculations. These techniques expand the kinds of questions SQL can answer without changing the fundamental analytical process: define the question, identify the necessary data, build the query, and examine what the results actually mean. In the next chapter, we will bring these skills together to solve practical problems involving customers, products, sales, marketing, expenses, and operations.

Chapter 6: Solving Real-World Data Analysis Problems

The SQL techniques covered throughout this book become most valuable when they are applied to actual questions. In a real analysis, you rarely use `SELECT`, JOINs, calculations, or window functions simply because they are available. You use them because someone needs to understand customers, evaluate sales, measure marketing performance, control expenses, or improve operations. This chapter brings those skills together by showing how analytical questions can be translated into practical SQL investigations and, ultimately, useful findings.

Analyzing Customers, Products, and Sales

Customer and sales data can answer some of the most important questions a business has.

Consider an `orders` table containing:

```
order_id | customer_id |
order_date | order_total
501      | 1001        |
2026-01-08 | 79.98
```

```
502         | 1002              |
2026-01-15 | 199.99
503         | 1001              |
2026-02-04 | 74.97
504         | 1003              |
2026-02-18 | 399.98
505         | 1001              |
2026-03-02 | 132.50
```

One useful question might be:

"Which customers generate the most revenue?"

We can calculate customer spending:

```
SELECT
    customer_id,
    COUNT(*) AS
number_of_orders,
    SUM(order_total) AS
total_spent
FROM orders
GROUP BY customer_id
ORDER BY total_spent DESC;
```

This query provides two useful measurements.

`COUNT(*)` shows how many orders each customer placed.

`SUM(order_total)` shows how much each customer spent.

These measurements reveal different behaviors. A customer might order frequently but make small purchases, while another might place fewer orders with much higher values.

We can also calculate average order value by customer:

```
SELECT
    customer_id,
    COUNT(*) AS
number_of_orders,
    SUM(order_total) AS
total_spent,
    AVG(order_total) AS
average_order_value
FROM orders
GROUP BY customer_id
ORDER BY total_spent DESC;
```

Now the analysis provides a more complete picture.

Products can be analyzed in a similar way.

Suppose an `order_items` table contains:

```
order_id | product_id | quantity
| unit_price
501      | 201        | 2
| 39.99
502      | 202        | 1
| 199.99
```

```
503         | 203             | 3
| 24.99
504         | 202             | 2
| 199.99
```

We can calculate product revenue:

```
SELECT
    product_id,
    SUM(quantity) AS units_sold,
    SUM(quantity * unit_price)
AS product_revenue
FROM order_items
GROUP BY product_id
ORDER BY product_revenue DESC;
```

This can help answer:

"Which products generate the most revenue?"

But notice that revenue and units sold are not necessarily the same measure of success.

A lower-priced product could sell many units while generating less revenue than a more expensive product.

That means a useful product analysis might compare:

```
Units sold
Revenue
Number of orders
Average selling price
```

```
Performance over time
```

We could also connect product information using a JOIN:

```
SELECT
    products.product_name,
    products.category,
    SUM(order_items.quantity) AS
units_sold,
    SUM(
        order_items.quantity *
order_items.unit_price
    ) AS product_revenue
FROM order_items
JOIN products
ON order_items.product_id =
products.product_id
GROUP BY products.product_id,
         products.product_name,
         products.category
ORDER BY product_revenue DESC;
```

The query now turns transaction records into a practical product-performance report.

Exploring Marketing, Expenses, and Operations

SQL analysis is not limited to sales.

Suppose a `marketing_campaigns` table contains:

```
campaign_id | channel        |
cost     | conversions
1          | Search         |
1200.00 | 48
2          | Social         |
900.00   | 30
3          | Email          |
250.00   | 42
4          | Display        |
750.00   | 15
```

We might want to know how much each conversion cost.

A **cost per conversion** calculation could be written as:

```
SELECT
    channel,
    cost,
    conversions,
    cost / NULLIF(conversions,
0) AS cost_per_conversion
FROM marketing_campaigns
ORDER BY cost_per_conversion;
```

`NULLIF()` helps avoid dividing by zero when a campaign has no conversions.

The analysis might reveal that one channel generates conversions at a much lower cost than another.

That does not automatically prove that the cheaper channel is better. Revenue, customer quality, repeat purchases, and other factors could also matter.

Again, SQL provides evidence. The analyst provides context.

Expense analysis follows the same principle.

Suppose we have:

```
expense_id | expense_date |
category    | amount
1           | 2026-01-05   |
Advertising | 850.00
2           | 2026-01-08   |
Software    | 275.00
3           | 2026-01-15   |
Shipping    | 425.00
4           | 2026-02-02   |
Advertising | 975.00
```

We could summarize expenses by category:

```
SELECT
    category,
    SUM(amount) AS total_expense
FROM expenses
GROUP BY category
```

```
ORDER BY total_expense DESC;
```

Or examine expenses by month:

```
SELECT
    strftime('%Y-%m',
expense_date) AS month,
    SUM(amount) AS
monthly_expense
FROM expenses
GROUP BY strftime('%Y-%m',
expense_date)
ORDER BY month;
```

Operations data can be approached in much the same way.

Imagine an inventory table:

```
product_id | quantity_on_hand |
reorder_level
201        | 25               |
10
202        | 6                |
10
203        | 14               |
8
204        | 4                |
12
```

We can identify products below their reorder level:

```
SELECT
```

```
    product_id,
    quantity_on_hand,
    reorder_level
FROM inventory
WHERE quantity_on_hand <
reorder_level;
```

This is a simple query, but it answers an operational question directly:

"Which products may need to be reordered?"

The same analytical approach can be used for many types of operational information:

```
Inventory levels
Shipping times
Order volumes
Processing times
Returns
Supplier activity
Staffing information
Production records
```

The subject changes, but the analytical process remains familiar.

Define what you need to understand, identify the relevant data, and construct a query that measures it.

Moving From SQL Results to Useful Insights and Decisions

A query result is not automatically an **insight**.

Suppose SQL tells us:

```
January revenue:  $85,000
February revenue: $91,000
March revenue:    $74,000
```

The result tells us what happened.

An analyst might observe:

"March revenue was lower than February revenue."

That is an observation.

The next question should be:

"Why?"

Perhaps the number of orders decreased.

We could investigate:

```
SELECT
    strftime('%Y-%m',
order_date) AS month,
    COUNT(*) AS
number_of_orders,
    SUM(order_total) AS revenue
FROM orders
GROUP BY strftime('%Y-%m',
order_date)
ORDER BY month;
```

Suppose the result shows:

```
month    | number_of_orders |
revenue
2026-01 | 520              |
85000
2026-02 | 550              |
91000
2026-03 | 545              |
74000
```

Order volume barely changed between February and March.

That suggests another possibility.

Perhaps customers spent less per order.

We could add:

```
SELECT
    strftime('%Y-%m',
order_date) AS month,
    COUNT(*) AS
number_of_orders,
    SUM(order_total) AS revenue,
    AVG(order_total) AS
average_order_value
FROM orders
GROUP BY strftime('%Y-%m',
order_date)
ORDER BY month;
```

Now suppose average order value fell substantially in March.

We have moved closer to understanding the change.

The analysis could continue by product:

```
SELECT
    products.product_name,
    SUM(order_items.quantity *
order_items.unit_price)
        AS product_revenue
FROM order_items
JOIN products
ON order_items.product_id =
products.product_id
GROUP BY products.product_id,
         products.product_name
ORDER BY product_revenue DESC;
```

Perhaps sales of several higher-priced products declined.

This illustrates an important analytical progression:

```
Result:
Revenue declined.

Question:
Why did revenue decline?

Investigation:
```

```
Check order volume.

Finding:
Order volume remained similar.

Next investigation:
Check average order value.

Finding:
Average order value declined.

Next investigation:
Examine product performance.
```

Data analysis is often a sequence of questions rather than one enormous query.

It is also important to distinguish **correlation** from causation.

Suppose advertising spending increased during the same months that revenue increased.

The data may show that the two moved together, but that alone does not prove the additional advertising caused the revenue increase.

Other factors could have contributed.

Similarly, an unusual result should be investigated before becoming the basis for a decision.

A useful workflow is:

```
Ask the question
        |
Write the query
        |
Check the data
        |
Review the result
        |
Ask follow-up questions
        |
Look for alternative
explanations
        |
Develop an insight
        |
Support a decision
```

SQL is powerful because it makes this investigation possible across datasets far larger than someone could reasonably inspect manually.

But SQL does not replace judgment.

The analyst still needs to understand what the measurements represent, recognize limitations in the available information, check whether the results make sense, and avoid making claims that the data cannot support.

That combination of technical skill and analytical thinking is what turns database records into useful information.

Last Thoughts

Real-world SQL analysis begins with a question and develops through investigation. Customer, product, sales, marketing, expense, and operational records can each reveal different parts of what is happening, but useful analysis requires choosing appropriate measurements and interpreting them in context. A result may lead to an observation, an observation may lead to another question, and several queries may be necessary before a meaningful insight emerges. The goal is not to write the most complicated SQL possible. It is to use the right query to understand the data well enough to support better questions, clearer conclusions, and more informed decisions.

Last Thoughts

Learning SQL for data analysis is not about memorizing every command available in the language. The more important skill is learning how to look at a collection of data, identify what you want to understand, and build a query that helps you investigate it. Throughout this book, you have moved from basic database structures and `SELECT` statements to filtering, calculations, JOINs, time-based analysis, advanced queries, and practical analytical problems. Those techniques provide a foundation you can continue applying to increasingly complex datasets.

Think in Questions, Not Just Queries

When you begin working with a database, it can be tempting to immediately start writing SQL.

A better starting point is the question.

Suppose you have a large sales database.

Instead of asking:

"What SQL should I write?"

Ask:

"What do I want to understand?"

Perhaps you want to know whether revenue is growing.

That question can be broken into smaller questions:

```
How much revenue was generated each month?

How does this month compare with the previous month?

Did the number of orders change?

Did average order value change?

Which products contributed most to the difference?
```

Each question gives your SQL a purpose.

You might begin with monthly revenue:

```
SELECT
    strftime('%Y-%m',
order_date) AS month,
    SUM(order_total) AS revenue
FROM orders
GROUP BY strftime('%Y-%m',
order_date)
ORDER BY month;
```

If revenue declined, that result creates another question.

You might investigate order volume:

```
SELECT
    strftime('%Y-%m',
order_date) AS month,
    COUNT(*) AS number_of_orders
FROM orders
GROUP BY strftime('%Y-%m',
order_date)
ORDER BY month;
```

Then perhaps average order value:

```
SELECT
    strftime('%Y-%m',
order_date) AS month,
    AVG(order_total) AS
average_order_value
FROM orders
GROUP BY strftime('%Y-%m',
order_date)
ORDER BY month;
```

This is analytical thinking in practice.

You are not writing queries simply to produce numbers. You are using each result to understand the problem more clearly.

A useful process to remember is:

```
Question
    |
```

```
Relevant Data
    |
SQL Query
    |
Result
    |
Interpretation
    |
Follow-Up Question
    |
Insight
```

Sometimes one query will provide the answer you need.

Other times, the first query will simply show you where to investigate next.

Both outcomes are useful.

Build SQL Skills Through Practical Analysis

One of the best ways to strengthen your SQL skills is to work with datasets that represent recognizable problems.

You do not need millions of records.

A small sales database can teach you how to calculate revenue.

A customer database can teach you how to group and compare customers.

An inventory database can teach you how to identify low-stock products.

An expense database can teach you how to summarize spending.

For example, create a simple orders table and begin with:

```
SELECT *
FROM orders;
```

Then ask increasingly useful questions.

How many orders are there?

```
SELECT COUNT(*) AS
number_of_orders
FROM orders;
```

How much revenue did they generate?

```
SELECT SUM(order_total) AS
total_revenue
FROM orders;
```

Which customers spent the most?

```
SELECT
    customer_id,
    SUM(order_total) AS
total_spent
```

```
FROM orders
GROUP BY customer_id
ORDER BY total_spent DESC;
```

How did revenue change by month?

```
SELECT
    strftime('%Y-%m',
order_date) AS month,
    SUM(order_total) AS revenue
FROM orders
GROUP BY strftime('%Y-%m',
order_date)
ORDER BY month;
```

You can continue expanding the same dataset as your skills improve.

Add customer information and practice JOINs.

Add products and analyze categories.

Add dates and examine trends.

Create CTEs to organize more complicated calculations.

Use window functions to create rankings and comparisons.

This approach gives each SQL technique a practical purpose.

It also helps you become comfortable checking your work.

If a query returns a result you did not expect, investigate it.

Look at the underlying records.

Check your JOIN conditions.

Review your filters.

Confirm that your groups represent what you intended to measure.

Compare calculated results with smaller samples when possible.

An important part of becoming better at SQL analysis is learning not only how to produce a result, but also how to determine whether that result makes sense.

Continuing Your Data Analysis Journey

SQL can take you surprisingly far in data analysis.

With the techniques covered in this book, you can retrieve information, filter records, summarize large datasets, compare groups, connect tables, investigate trends, calculate KPIs, rank results, and answer practical questions.

Your next step does not need to be learning every advanced SQL feature.

Instead, continue building depth around the analytical process.

Practice moving from:

`"What data do I have?"`

to:

`"What can this data actually tell me?"`

Then move toward:

`"What additional questions should I ask?"`

As your experience grows, you may encounter larger databases, more complicated table relationships, and analytical questions requiring several stages of calculation.

You may also begin combining SQL with other analytical tools.

SQL might retrieve and prepare the necessary information from a database, while spreadsheet software, visualization tools, statistical software, or programming languages can be used for additional analysis and presentation.

But SQL remains valuable because so much organizational information is stored in relational databases.

The ability to independently ask a database a question can change the way you work with information.

Instead of waiting for a prepared report, you can investigate.

Instead of looking only at totals, you can explore what created them.

Instead of accepting an unusual result immediately, you can examine the underlying records.

And instead of treating data as a collection of numbers, you can begin treating it as evidence that can help answer questions.

Last Thoughts

The most valuable lesson in SQL data analysis is simple: **start with the question**. Understand what you are trying to learn, identify the data that can help, write a query that measures the right thing, and examine the result carefully. Then ask another question if necessary. SQL gives you the technical ability to search, combine, calculate, and compare information, but analytical thinking determines whether those results become useful insights. Continue practicing with real datasets and practical questions, and the commands covered in this book will gradually become something more valuable than syntax: a repeatable way to investigate data and understand what it is telling you.

Glossary

Aggregate Function: A SQL function that performs a calculation across multiple records and returns a summarized result. Common examples include `COUNT()`, `SUM()`, `AVG()`, `MIN()`, and `MAX()`.

Alias: A temporary name assigned to a column, table, or calculated result within a SQL query, commonly using `AS`.

Analytical Mindset: An approach to data that begins with a clear question, examines relevant evidence, checks assumptions, and uses results to develop useful conclusions or additional questions.

ASC: Short for ascending. Used with `ORDER BY` to arrange values from lowest to highest, earliest to latest, or alphabetically.

AVG(): An aggregate function used to calculate the average of a group of numerical values.

Business Question: A practical question about performance, customers, products, operations, expenses, or another area that can potentially be investigated using data.

Calculated Value: A value created within a SQL query using existing data, such as multiplying quantity by unit price to calculate revenue.

CASE: A SQL expression that applies conditional logic and returns different values depending on whether specified conditions are met.

Column: A field in a database table representing a particular type of information, such as customer name, revenue, product category, or order date.

Common Table Expression (CTE): A temporary named result created with `WITH` that can make complex SQL queries easier to organize and understand.

Correlation: A relationship in which two measurements appear to change together. Correlation alone does not prove that one caused the other.

COUNT(): An aggregate function used to count records or values.

Data Analysis: The process of examining data to answer questions, make comparisons, identify patterns, calculate measurements, and develop useful insights.

Data Quality: The overall condition and reliability of data, including considerations such as completeness, consistency, accuracy, duplicates, and missing information.

Data Type: A classification describing the type of information stored in a database field, such as integer, text, date, or decimal values.

Database: An organized collection of information that can be stored, retrieved, updated, and analyzed.

DESC: Short for descending. Used with `ORDER BY` to arrange values from highest to lowest, latest to earliest, or reverse alphabetical order.

DISTINCT: A SQL keyword used to return unique values while removing repeated values from query results.

Filter: A condition used to narrow a dataset so that only records meeting particular requirements are included.

Foreign Key: A field in one table that references a related record in another table.

GROUP BY: A SQL clause used to organize records into groups so calculations can be performed for each group.

HAVING: A SQL clause used to filter grouped or aggregated results.

INNER JOIN: A JOIN that returns records when matching values exist in both related tables.

Insight: A meaningful understanding developed by interpreting analytical results in context, rather than simply reporting a number or observation.

JOIN: A SQL operation used to combine related information from two or more database tables.

Key Performance Indicator (KPI): A measurement used to evaluate a particular aspect of performance, such as revenue, average order value, conversion rate, or units sold.

LAG(): A window function that allows a query to access a value from a previous row, making it useful for period-to-period comparisons.

LEFT JOIN: A JOIN that returns all records from the left table along with matching records from the related table. Records from the left table can remain even when no match exists.

LIKE: A SQL operator used to search for text that matches a specified pattern.

LIMIT: A SQL clause used in many database systems to restrict the number of records returned by a query.

MAX(): An aggregate function used to find the highest value in a group.

MIN(): An aggregate function used to find the lowest value in a group.

NULL: A database value representing missing, unknown, or unavailable information.

NULLIF(): A SQL function that returns NULL when two expressions are equal. It can be useful for preventing calculations such as division by zero.

Observation: Something directly noticed in analytical results, such as revenue being lower in March than in February. An observation does not necessarily explain why something happened.

ORDER BY: A SQL clause used to sort query results according to one or more columns or calculated values.

PARTITION BY: A component commonly used with window functions to divide records into separate groups for analytical calculations without collapsing the individual rows.

Primary Key: A field used to uniquely identify each record in a database table.

Query: A request or instruction sent to a database to retrieve, filter, calculate, combine, or otherwise work with information.

RANK(): A window function used to assign rankings to records based on a specified order.

Relational Database: A database that organizes information into tables that can be connected through relationships between fields.

Row: A single record in a database table.

SELECT: The SQL command used to retrieve specified information from a database.

SQL: Structured Query Language, a language used to communicate with relational databases and retrieve, organize, calculate, and analyze stored information.

Subquery: A SQL query placed inside another query so the result of one calculation or retrieval can be used by another.

SUM(): An aggregate function used to calculate the total of numerical values.

Table: A database structure that organizes related information into rows and columns.

Table Relationship: A connection between tables based on related fields, such as connecting customers and orders through `customer_id`.

Time-Series Analysis: The examination of measurements across time to identify changes, trends, patterns, or differences between periods.

WHERE: A SQL clause used to filter individual records according to specified conditions.

Window Function: A SQL function that performs calculations across related rows while preserving individual records in the query results.

WITH: The SQL keyword commonly used to begin a Common Table Expression.

About the Author

Roggie "Raj" Clark is an entrepreneur and a 10-year marketing professional with a proven track record in e-commerce and digital business growth. Having built and managed successful online stores with thousands of sales and consulted for numerous marketing clients, Roggie has mastered the intricacies of online marketing, branding, and consumer behavior. He has also written several popular books on digital marketing, SEO (search engine optimization), and programming (HTML, CSS, and JavaScript).

As a former marketing manager at a fintech company—a role he secured through his own marketing and financial expertise—Roggie gained firsthand experience in financial strategy and wealth-building. This journey inspired him to share insights with amateur investors, helping them save money, make smarter financial decisions, and build long-term wealth. Raj currently lives in Maryland with his sister and niece.

www.ingramcontent.com/pod-product-compliance
Lightning Source LLC
LaVergne TN
LVHW050825061126
851857LV00012B/981
* 9 7 9 8 2 4 0 8 0 4 9 4 6 *